EATING SALAD DRUNK

EATING SALAD DRUNK

HAIKUS FOR THE BURNOUT AGE
BY COMEDY GREATS

EDITED BY GABE HENRY

Illustrations by Emily Flake
Foreword by Aparna Nancherla

ST. MARTIN'S
GRIFFIN
New York

First published in the United States by St. Martin's Griffin,
an imprint of St. Martin's Publishing Group

EATING SALAD DRUNK. Copyright © 2021 by Gabe Henry. Foreword
copyright © 2021 by Aparna Nancherla. Illustrations copyright
© 2021 by Emily Flake. All rights reserved. Printed in the United
States of America. For information, address St. Martin's Publishing
Group, 120 Broadway, New York, NY 10271.

www.stmartins.com

Design by Donna Sinisgalli Noetzel

Library of Congress Cataloging-in-Publication Data

Names: Henry, Gabe, editor. | Flake, Emily, 1977– illustrator. |
    Nancherla, Aparna, writer of foreword.
Title: Eating salad drunk : haikus for the burnout age by comedy
    greats / edited by Gabe Henry ; illustrations by Emily Flake ;
    foreword by Aparna Nancherla.
Description: First edition. | New York : St. Martin's Griffin, 2021.
Identifiers: LCCN 2021015951 | ISBN 9781250774217 (paper
    over board) | ISBN 9781250774224 (ebook)
Subjects: LCSH: Haiku, American. | Humorous poetry,
    American. | American wit and humor.
Classification: LCC PS593.H3 E18 2021 | DDC
    811/.04108170905—dcundefined
LC record available at https://lccn.loc.gov/2021015951

Our books may be purchased in bulk for promotional, educational,
or business use. Please contact your local bookseller or the
Macmillan Corporate and Premium Sales Department at
1-800-221-7945, extension 5442, or by email at
MacmillanSpecialMarkets@macmillan.com.

First Edition: 2021

10 9 8 7 6 5 4 3 2 1

TO CELINA, NORA, AND DANNY

CONTENTS

Sasheer Zamata • Maria Bamford • Emmy Blotnick • Jo Firestone • Mike DiCenzo • Rosebud Baker • Christian Finnegan • Myq Kaplan • Ophira Eisenberg • Mike Birbiglia • Jean Grae • Jes Tom • Aparna Nancherla • Flula Borg • Ian Fidance • Laura Silverman

FRIENDS & FAMILY 59

Ariel Dumas • Myq Kaplan • Maria Bamford • Cathy Humes • Giulia Rozzi • Josh Comers • Margaret Cho • Anna Drezen • Leo Allen • Liz Magee • Luke Mones • Alonzo Bodden • Jes Tom • Ophira Eisenberg • Matthew Broussard • Nick Vatterott • Chloe Radcliffe • Atsuko Okatsuka

MODERN ROMANCE 77

Kyle Ayers • Scott Rogowsky • Steve Mittleman • Kevin Smith • Joe Zimmerman • Demi Adejuyigbe • Erica Rhodes • Kelly Bachman • Giulia Rozzi • Christi Chiello • Jes Tom • Catherine Cohen • Myka Fox • Josh Comers • Laura Silverman • Myq Kaplan • Martin Urbano • Sierra Katow • Ariel Elias • Erin Jackson • Beth Stelling

THE STRUGGLE IS REAL 103

Ziwe Fumudoh • Alyssa Limperis • Karen Chee • Ophira Eisenberg • Ayo Edebiri • Dave Holmes • Atsuko Okatsuka • Natasha Vaynblat • Colin Mochrie • Sierra Katow • Kelly

A joke [is] the minimum amount of words to get to a punch line.

—RICKY GERVAIS

FOREWORD

When I was invited to write a foreword to a book of haikus written by comedians, I'll be honest, I thought the assignment would max out at three lines, seventeen syllables. Alas, like most jobs I get, I vastly misinterpreted what was being asked of me.

To be fair though, that's also my stand-up comic brain kicking in because, as a species, we jesters generally try to keep our ideas on the shorter side. Get in, get out, leave 'em wanting more. Nobody ever says about a great joke they're trying to recall, "Hold on, let me just get my pages in order here."

I once had a colleague listen to one of my jokes and then suggest dropping two words from it. I, of course, reacted nothing but gracefully—smiled to his face, seethed inside, plotted my revenge—because not only are comedians the epitome of hypersensitive artist types, but we cannot believe someone we personally know would have the nerve to give us less than glowing feedback. I tried the joke his way a couple times, and guess the hell what? It worked better. Not that he'll ever know! He's dead (to me)—but see? We're always editing even when it's not our stuff. The comedian's motto is basically, "Life is short, get to the point."

That's the beauty of the haiku. Like a good stand-up joke, a haiku needs to be boiled down to the sharpest little nugget at the heart of it. (Did you enjoy my apt analogy about boiling the hearts of sharp little nuggets? So relatable!) The more precise and specific a setup you craft, the more satisfying the surprise of the punch line. In comedy, even if the final bit ends up being much longer, it is comprised of many individual jokes, each of which you try to make as "tight" as possible—meaning stripped of all unnecessary fluff. (For example, that last sentence back there? Not tight!) That's why comedians are always talking about their tight fives versus their loose tens. A loose ten might mean one minute of good material and nine minutes of dissociative rambling. Nobody's impressed.

Tweets, 'grams, Snapchats, and TikToks—it seems everything these days can be boiled down to a few seconds or a minute of commitment as a consumer. This twenty-three-second clip of the latest Supreme Court hearing set to the *Family Matters* theme song is king, until two hours* later when this new tweet clapback from Adele to Big Oil is making the "this wins everything" rounds. Not only is the amount of available content now at an all-time high, but the natural human desire for novelty makes everybody want to switch topics constantly. I'm not sure what this says about the future of society as we know it, because I already forgot what we were talking about, but one thing's for sure, if you want to grab focus these days, you better steer clear of TL;DR territory (what ancient societies used to call "too long; didn't read").

So sit back, relax, and enjoy these little comedic nuggets! Appreciate not only the words you read, but also the words

---

*Twenty minutes is the new hour. Please share, like, and subscribe.

you *don't* read, like . . . jazz. (Did I just compare yet another thing to jazz? Yes, yes, I did.) And congratulations, this is the longest amount of text you'll have to see in this entire book. That's the true beauty of the haiku. You'll never feel more accomplished as a reader . . . cough, ahem, cough . . . I meant micro-book-influencer.

—APARNA NANCHERLA, 2021

INTRODUCTION

Sometime around the turn of the sixteenth century, in the hills of central Japan, a Buddhist monk emerged from his seclusion, knelt before the bed of his ailing father, and composed a verse so full of worldly wisdom that it stuns us yet today:

> Even at the time
> When my father lay dying
> I still kept farting.

The author of this flatulent ode, Yamazaki Sōkan, was one of the founders of *haikai*—the forerunner and namesake of haiku poetry—and this poem was among the world's very first haikus.

There's a lot we English-speaking moderns don't understand (and misunderstand) about haiku poetry, but perhaps our greatest error is thinking that haikus need to be *serious.* From its earliest days, the heart of haiku poetry was *humor.* These three-line, seventeen-syllable poems—composed communally and in the informal, everyday language of Japan's lower class—tended toward the lewd and crude, the comical and lighthearted, and poets like Yamazaki Sōkan were as likely to wax poetic about ponds and dewdrops as they were about excrement and urination. (Nature is nature, after all.) The roots of the haiku, in fact, are right there in the word itself: *haikai* literally means "comic verse."

My own association with haiku humor began the very day I learned what a haiku was. It was freshman year of high school. I was sitting in the back of English class, steeling myself for another dreary analysis of *Wuthering Heights,* when Ms. Connolly brought out a laminated poster printed with a three-line poem and tacked it on the wall. It was National Haiku Day, she explained, and today we would all try our hand at poetry.

The rules of the form were simple: three unrhymed lines of five, seven, and five syllables each. If Ms. Connolly—bless her heart—thought this exercise might lull us into a state of Zen relaxation, thereby buying her an hour's peace and quiet, she was certainly disappointed. It exploded instead into a rowdy competition, with all the aspiring class clowns trying to outwit each other in three-line, seventeen-syllable bursts. Before long, we had taken this peaceful poetic form to where adolescent boys inevitably take all things: the offensive, gross, and scatological.

In a moment of divine inspiration (with a hint of bowel discomfort), I wrote this gem:

> I stare at the clock
> Waiting for the bell, so I
> Can finally poop.

With a better understanding of haiku history, Ms. Connolly might have bestowed upon us all bonus points for channeling the great Sōkan. Instead we got pop quizzes every day for the next week.

Stand-up comedy and haiku poetry—two art forms separated by continents and centuries—have more in common than one might think. Both rely foremost on concision: Each word must be arranged in the right syllabic rhythm, with the perfect beat and punch, for the work to be effective. (Rodney Dangerfield would have been a great haiku poet. So would Mitch Hedberg.) Both employ wordplay: Traditional Japanese haiku poets leaned heavily on double entendre and puns. (Nishiyama Sōin was particularly fond of the phrase *tsuki idete*, which could mean either *moon* or *erection*, depending on the context.) And both abide (loosely) by the Rule of Three, a principle that holds that things that come in *threes* are inherently funnier or more compelling than items in other denominations: the Three Stooges, Three Amigos, Goldilocks and the Three Bears, and just about every bar joke you've ever heard (a blonde, a brunette, and a redhead; a priest, a rabbi, and a minister).

In joke telling, this three-item rule usually takes the form of two set-up lines followed by a punch line. Take this haiku by the New York comedian Myq Kaplan:

Star Wars. Star Trek. Dune.
Battlestar Galactica.
Girls don't sleep with me.

Or this by the legendary Elayne Boosler:

Thought I saw Groucho.
Moustache, glasses, funny walk.
Close, but no cigar.

Or this shameful confession from Ray Romano:

Just killed a spider.
Didn't have to, but he saw
Me masturbating.

A teacher friend of mine once told me that when she teaches haiku, she has her students cut out "haiku glasses" from cardboard tubes; by peering through these cylinders at a patch of grass, a leaf, a puddle, the field of view is restricted, and the observer can focus on a small, contained area. Jerry Seinfeld may as well be looking through a cardboard tube when he tunnel-focuses on a hair on the bathroom wall, or the top button of a collared shirt, or the buckle on an airplane seatbelt. Sometimes comedy expands our scope to highlight profound truths about life and the cosmos; other times it narrows our view to the infinitesimal, the everyday, the subtle, and the subtly irritating. Observational humor contains the essence of haiku. It is comedy through a cardboard tube.

Strangely enough, there seems to be no better poetry for our burnout age than this five-century-old Japanese triplet. Haikus are the world's shortest poems—snapshots of the world in its smallest distillations—and we are a generation that requires its information short and distilled. (And snapshotted, too, if possible, with a Juno filter please). With platforms like Twitter restricting the space in which we convey and consume our world, and traditional media rushing to meet our ever-shrinking capacity to concentrate, we now expect everything in bite-sized, meme-ified form. Haikus, in their brevity and appeal to the attention-deprived, may just be the poetry for these times.

To my delight, nearly every comedian I approached for this book was not only receptive but breathlessly eager to contribute. As I learned years ago in Ms. Connolly's class, there is something addictive about writing within constraint. It brings out a creative ingenuity in the artist—a personal challenge to see how much can be done in a limited space. (Just think how much came out of Shakespeare's ten-syllables-per-line iambic constraints, or Hemingway's six-word-story challenge.) The challenge: Can you write a self-contained joke or bit using only seventeen syllables? And once I opened the tap, I couldn't stop it. The haikus poured in.

I hope you enjoy reading these little droplets of wit and crudity as much as I've enjoyed collecting them. And I hope you find that this Zen poetry we call *haiku*—ancient and outmoded though it may seem—fits remarkably well in today's fast-paced, short-spaced era of Twitter, TikTok, and dwindling attention spans. To quote one modern haiku master:

Who has time for more
Than seventeen syllables
These days anyway?

—GABE HENRY, EDITOR AND CURATOR

SCREEN TIME

"I'm huge on Twitter."

—An ancient proverb that means

Lonely in real life.

—JOEL KIM BOOSTER

Feeling confident
Until I log on to Zoom.
Is that my real face?

—OPHIRA EISENBERG

Accidentally

FaceTimed my doctor's office.

The call was declined.

—APARNA NANCHERLA

Any adult who
Uses Snapchat probably
Has a coke problem.

—HANNA DICKINSON

Every morning I
Wake up depressed knowing that
TikTok is a thing.

—SCOTT ROGOWSKY

The dogs I follow

On Instagram have better

Lives than most of us.

—SIERRA KATOW

Tweet, tweet, tweet some more.

Gobble up those followers.

Is there more to life?

—SEAN PATTON

"Per my last email"
Is just me being polite.
Fuckin REPLY NOW.

—KYLE AYERS

"Sorry, just saw this!"
He says, and I believe him
Because I want to.

—KAREN CHEE

—MICHAEL IAN BLACK

How many minutes
Must I wait to like a post
To not seem thirsty?

—SIERRA KATOW

Can we use "hashtag"

To describe when someone throws

Potatoes at brunch?

—NATASHA VAYNBLAT

How many times will
I search "add thingy to e"?
You just hold down é.

—JOE ZIMMERMAN

What is a haiku?
How many syllables per—

. . . Siri, what is a

—ZACH WOODS

The showbiz bigwigs

Will be sorry when I go

Viral on TikTok.

—DINA HASHEM

A sword is mighty.

A pen, mightier. Best move:

Tweet the company.

—ROY WOOD JR.

To the man reading
A book on the train: You think
You're *better* than us??

—CHLOE RADCLIFFE

Podcast, oh podcast.

Copilot of my commute.

My only true friend.

—AMANDA LUND

A word of advice?
Get off social media
It makes kids Nazis.

—JENA FRIEDMAN

Emperor Facebook:
Bless my growth, reach, engagement.
Ticket sales are low.

—DINA HASHEM

The military

Is training teens through TikTok

For the dance army.

—NATASHA VAYNBLAT

My sleep-tracking app
Says I lose the most sleep when
I check my sleep app.

—CHLOE RADCLIFFE

"Human connection
Is what life is all about"
She typed on her phone.

—AMANDA LUND

When I die, someone

Scroll through my Netflix for me.

It likes the scrolling.

—KYLE AYERS

People on Twitter
Seem chill considering they
Ate glass for breakfast.

—ROSEBUD BAKER

Got to the end of
The internet. Turns out I
Was dead the whole time.

—APARNA NANCHERLA

FOOD

My mom could cook well.
My dad could be tried at the
Hague for cuisine crimes.

—GREG PROOPS

Expiration dates

Don't exist in my mom's house.

"Those are suggestions!"

—ALYSSA LIMPERIS

Eating salad drunk

Is both irresponsible

And responsible.

—JOSH GONDELMAN

Oh, back-right oven

Burner. I am sorry I

Will never use you.

—KYLE AYERS

A hotel breakfast

Fruit, yogurt, and piece of toast.

"I'm Continental!"

—ROBERT DEAN

Hunched over the sink
Eating spaghetti. Sure, a
Colander's a bowl.

—BRETT DAVIS

Eggs, flour, and salt.
All you need to make pasta.
For real. Google it.

—JENA FRIEDMAN

Spaghetti is one-

Dimensional linguine

Trying to fool you.

—WYATT CENAC

Eggs over easy

Always has the appearance

Of a murder scene.

—JERRY SEINFELD

Bad news. Doctor says

I must stop eating bacon

During my checkups.

—GEORGE WALLACE

I want to start a

Butt-shaped cookie company

Called "Damn, Dat Ass Dough."

—GIULIA ROZZI

"I am not hungry."
Is a sentence we don't have
In the Greek language.

—ALYSSA LIMPERIS

Texas without its
Mexican food is really
Just Oklahoma.

—GREG PROOPS

I'll eat a skirt steak
While wearing a pair of pants.
I don't give a shit.

—GEORGE WALLACE

Don't eat that jerky
Until you make sure it's not
A piece of Band-Aid.

—CATHY HUMES

Tried to go vegan

But not for the animals.

Vegans just look hot.

—SASHEER ZAMATA

If I stop eating

Sugar, would I ever stop

Talking about it?

—MARIA BAMFORD

One thing I won't share?
My secret eggs recipe.
Oh shit, I said "eggs."

—EMMY BLOTNICK

Here's my impression

Of some microwave popcorn:

Pop-pop-pop.... pop................ pop.

—JO FIRESTONE

AND

MIKE DICENZO

Eating dairy gives

Me hives, but I won't just QUIT.

That's not how LOVE works.

—ROSEBUD BAKER

You guys, I did it.

Hot dogs with Goldfish crackers.

The saddest dinner.

—CHRISTIAN FINNEGAN

Cafeteria.

Café plus bacteria?

I will eat at home.

—MYQ KAPLAN

She ate Nutella

Not knowing it'd stay on her

Chin through two meetings.

—JO FIRESTONE

I am on the couch

But my brain is in the fridge

With the chocolate.

—OPHIRA EISENBERG

Suck on a peanut

M&M long enough and

It's just a peanut.

—MIKE BIRBIGLIA

"Free refills of wine!!!"

That's the end of my TED Talk.

Thanks for coming, y'all.

—JEAN GRAE

23andMe

But for the Colonel's secret

Chicken recipe.

—JES TOM

All bananas have

Three settings: Unripe, Ripe, and

Class Action Lawsuit.

—APARNA NANCHERLA

Oh, Fruit by the Foot.

You flout the metric system

In a tasty way.

—JO FIRESTONE

AND

MIKE DICENZO

Hot French press coffee:
You make me warm during my
Underwear breakfast.

—FLULA BORG

I limit myself
To one cup of coffee each
Five to ten minutes.

—ALYSSA LIMPERIS

Every morning I

Drink a pot of coffee and

Promptly shit myself.

—IAN FIDANCE

A raccoon broke in!

Tore open Raisin Bran box!!

...I am the raccoon.

—MARIA BAMFORD

I chew on my ice
To let people know, if pushed,
I'd do this to bones.

—JO FIRESTONE

AND

MIKE DICENZO

Three in the morning
Refrigerator's humming.
Must not know the words.

—LAURA SILVERMAN

"*Wert wern*," said the duck.

He was simply trying to

Order a white wine.

—EMMY BLOTNICK

FRIENDS & FAMILY

Farewell to Grandma.

She died doing what she loved:

Teasing local bears.

—ARIEL DUMAS

"Happy Father's Day!"
Is not what you want to hear
If you did not know.

—MYQ KAPLAN

I'm a good kid. I

Take Mom to chemo. She sighs:

"Honey, your breath stinks."

—MARIA BAMFORD

I really like kids.

Favorite thing about them?

None of them are mine.

—CATHY HUMES

When my Wi-Fi says
It cannot connect I'm like
Are you my father?

—GIULIA ROZZI

Son's first to-do list:

Count to five. Sing alphabet.

Kill Dad. Marry Mom.

—JOSH COMERS

There's no greater joy
Than sloppy wet kisses from
A Chihuahua mouth.

My dog just farted.

On my pants. Then licked her butt.

Then licked my pants. Queen!

—ANNA DREZEN

Don't know about much
But I *do* know about Art.
(He's my uncle's friend.)

—LEO ALLEN

Happy birthday, friend!
Posted a pic where I look
Great and you look fine.

—LIZ MAGEE

My name is Luke but

My friends call me once every

Five to seven years.

—LUKE MONES

Dance like no one sees.

Sing like no one hears. Moral:

Don't have a roommate.

—ALONZO BODDEN

Dear roommates: please don't
Look in the pot on the stove.
I'm boiling dildos.

—JES TOM

I just want a house
Big enough to avoid the
People I live with.

—OPHIRA EISENBERG

The phrase "No homo"
Sounds like a nice neighborhood
North of SoHoMo.

—MATTHEW BROUSSARD

No man's an island
But Dad in the kiddie pool
Is pretty damn close.

—NICK VATTEROTT

Buying gifts for Dad
Is just buying gifts for *me*
But on layaway.

—CHLOE RADCLIFFE

"Oh, you know Bobby?"

I point out airplane window.

"Wow. What a small world."

—NICK VATTEROTT

"Don't worry, he's cool"
Is a bad way to describe
Your youth pastor friend.

—ATSUKO OKATSUKA

MODERN ROMANCE

Shall I compare thee
To a summer's day? I think
You are kinda hot.

—KYLE AYERS

Having girl problems?
Take comfort knowing you have
Jay Z's sympathies.

—SCOTT ROGOWSKY

I'm the silent type.

She's the silent treatment type.

We both nod a lot.

—STEVE MITTLEMAN

Tonight you taught me
It's wrong to like a movie
That you do not like.

—KEVIN SMITH

What you said to me
When I wasn't listening
Makes a lot of sense.

—JOE ZIMMERMAN

Long-distance dating
Works best when your love language
Is Southwest Air Miles.

—DEMI ADEJUYIGBE

Long-distance love is
Not really worth it if he's
In another world.

—ERICA RHODES

My last one-night stand
Paid for my dog's surgery
But not my Plan B.

—KELLY BACHMAN

I have been fucking

A broken marionette

With no strings attached.

—GIULIA ROZZI

I loved dry humping
So much that I was sad to
Try regular humps.

—CHRISTI CHIELLO

I only listen
To songs that made me horny
In 2008.

—JES TOM

Birth control is free.

Taco Bell delivers now.

Girls *can* have it all!

—CATHERINE COHEN

How to get your man
To do push-ups: Do push-ups
In front of him wrong.

—MYKA FOX

My dominatrix
Does not make it easy to
Reset your safe word.

—JOSH COMERS

A "tight five" is a
Stand-up set, or a new name
For fisting. You choose.

—JES TOM

My ex eats ass now.
Somehow that hurts way more than
All of his success.

—KELLY BACHMAN

I knew not of pain
Till I buried my true love
As they say, "alive."

—LAURA SILVERMAN

Necrophilia

Is not what I thought it was.

I like sex with necks.

—MYQ KAPLAN

My girlfriend and I

Have a whole lot in common

Genetically.

—MARTIN URBANO

.

It is better to

Have swiped and missed than never

To have swiped at all.

—SIERRA KATOW

Do anti-vaxxers

Have their own dating websites?

Hot shingles near you!

—ARIEL ELIAS

I just got felt up.

My bra triggered the alarm.

Was it good for you?

—ERIN JACKSON

The PC police

And the PC FBI

Seized all my hard drives.

—MARTIN URBANO

She sits down to write.

Just then a ping distracts her.

The *fuck* did he say?!

—BETH STELLING

THE STRUGGLE IS REAL

Do I Feel Like Doing Anything?

no no no no no

no no no no no no no

no no no no no

—ZIWE FUMUDOH

It's a lovely day

To go for a run! I should

Tell my friend who runs.

—ALYSSA LIMPERIS

Paul McCartney heard

"Yesterday" in a dream. I

Just hear "Not today!"

—KAREN CHEE

I recently learned:

Given all the time to write,

I still won't do it.

—OPHIRA EISENBERG

There's nothing sadder

Than writing a haiku and

Getting writer's block.

—AYO EDEBIRI

My finest acting:
When I leave a tiny store
Having bought nothing.

—DAVE HOLMES

Bought avocados.
Eleven organic ones.
Now I can't pay rent.

—ATSUKO OKATSUKA

It's hard to find good
Underwear when you steal it
From the laundromat.

—NATASHA VAYNBLAT

Doctors always say
Just listen to your body.
Mine screams constantly.

—COLIN MOCHRIE

Therapy's not cheap
But neither are the weighted
Plush sloths I buy drunk.

—SIERRA KATOW

My white therapist
Sent me a black emoji.
I can't pay her now.

—KELLY BACHMAN

I order five books

While I am reading one book.

I then read no books.

—IAN FIDANCE

Love when books have pics
In the middle. They're saying
"Take a break, big guy!"

—LUKE MONES

Did not exercise.
Wait, but I did change my sheets.
So yes, yes I did.

—LIZ MAGEE

I'm sorry I'm late!

The truth is I didn't want

To come here at all.

—ERICA RHODES

Partying in my
Thirties means leaving early
Because I had cheese.

—NATASHA VAYNBLAT

I stare at the wall.

I know I forgot something.

Oh . . .

. . . Happy birthday.

—AUBREY PLAZA

Daylight savings time:

The best excuse for being

Five hours late to work.

—JOE ZIMMERMAN

Been putting off work

To watch videos about

Procrastination.

—JIM TEWS

Can I report a

Hostile work environment

If I'm self-employed?

—ERICA RHODES

NATURE CALLS

Sprinkling sounds of rain

Do trigger bladder pressures.

Nature, you call me.

—FLULA BORG

The spring flowers bloom.

I cannot smell them because

Uncle has my nose.

—ROBERT DEAN

It's so cold—you can

See your breath go, "I'm leaving,

This body sucksssss."

—APARNA NANCHERLA

If you hold a shell
Up to your ear, you can hear
How lonely you are.

—EMMY BLOTNICK

Look at the night sky.
Stars look small, but we all know
They are fat AF.

—DINA HASHEM

Strawberry Moon: I
Don't care about your color
As much as your juice.

—AUBREY PLAZA

Unicorns are loved
But narwhals really exist
And nobody cares.

—LIZ MAGEE

Coyotes are dogs
With a bad case of toxic
Masculinity.

—AMY SILVERBERG

It's strange that a dog

Will eat a dead bird but will

Never eat a grape.

—TOM WILSON

Dog poop in the snow.

Someone needs to pick you up

You do not melt so.

—APARNA NANCHERLA

I love winter coats

That go down to my ankles.

I am free to fart.

—NATASHA VAYNBLAT

Love when a man cries

Almost as much as I love

When a woman farts.

—GIULIA ROZZI

To the man who farts

While listening to headphones:

Don't think we don't know.

—DAVE HILL

Summer in New York
Starts the first day that you smell
Garbage you can't see.

—JOSH GONDELMAN

The full moon rises.

A city sleeps peacefully.

Rats rats rats rats rats.

—AUBREY PLAZA

"Bug Bites on My Face:
A Makeup Tutorial."
(Nature's contouring.)

—APARNA NANCHERLA

Can crickets applaud?
Or can they just make the sound
Of "This is Boring"?

—ROBERT DEAN

ENTERTAINMENT

I know a show's great

When I only pause to text

Like, four or five times.

—DEMI ADEJUYIGBE

Let's talk TV shows.
Of all the big finales
Sopranos was the—

—MATT GOURLEY

Why can't we condense
David Byrne and David Lynch
Into just one guy?

—JOSH GONDELMAN

Life is way too short

To contradict a stranger

About liking *Clerks*.

—KEVIN SMITH

Star Wars. Star Trek. Dune.

Battlestar Galactica.

Girls don't sleep with me.

—MYQ KAPLAN

Seems about time for
A new Joker movie, right?
It's been a few months?

—KYLE AYERS

How bad is the pay
To be a superhero?
They all have day jobs.

—ARIEL ELIAS

I blame *Aladdin*

For half the homeless guys I've

Been attracted to.

—ARIEL ELIAS

Thought I saw Groucho.

Moustache, glasses, funny walk.

Close, but no cigar.

—ELAYNE BOOSLER

Shoot the show for months.

Talk about the show for years.

Binge it in a day.

—BOB ODENKIRK

All NPR hosts
Say their names as if they are
Apologizing.

—DAVE HOLMES

Imagine my grief
When I learned *Beat Bobby Flay*
Is about cooking.

—ARIEL DUMAS

I think the people
Surveyed on *Family Feud*
Must not get out much.

—ABBI CRUTCHFIELD

I want a rom-com

Where he puts her glasses ON

Because she's squinting.

—LIZ MAGEE

"Hey! Milton Bradley?
Why, it's the Parker Brothers!"
(Game recognize game.)

—NICK VATTEROTT

When I hear the word
"Algorithm" I picture
Al Gore swing dancing.

—GIULIA ROZZI

There was that summer.

We all just loved Jack Johnson.

I hope he's ok.

—KYLE AYERS

They're called "Real Housewives"
But not everyone's married.
And none to a house.

—ARIEL DUMAS

Frankenstein's Monster
Is more afraid of fire
Than a misnomer.

—ROBERT DEAN

'90s Kid

Everyday I think:
"Will this be the day that I
Get randomly slimed??"

—NATASHA VAYNBLAT

"Fuck, Marry, Kill: The
O. J. Simpson Story." Next
On ESPN.

—MYKA FOX

WORDS OF WISDOM

Not listening is

Crucial if you're going to

Be right all the time.

—ROSEBUD BAKER

People who live in

Glass houses shouldn't throw stones

Unless they're renting.

—PAUL LANDER

What's potted lip balm?
Just ChapStick with my dirty
Fingers up in it.

—KURT BRAUNOHLER

Hotel check-in is
All about getting briefed on
What a hotel is.

—LUKE MONES

Mimosa is French
For "drunk girls crying before
Noon on a Sunday."

—GIULIA ROZZI

If puppets were real

All they would talk about is

The hand up their ass.

—ROBERT DEAN

Have we figured out

If a woodchuck can chuck wood?

Asking for a friend.

—IRENE TU

My philosophy
Degree means even less now
That Reddit knows all.

—DINA HASHEM

As an optimist
I believe in living life
To the half-fullest.

—LAURA SILVERMAN

I don't see gender.

I don't see color either.

Letters are hard, too.

—DEMI ADEJUYIGBE

Is my toilet mad

When I pee in it at night?

Does it sleep then, too?

—EVA VICTOR

I don't know who needs
To hear this but your shower
Is not a toilet.

—ABBI CRUTCHFIELD

A pack of Wet Ones

Inadequately sealed shut

Is pack of Dry Ones.

—LAURA SILVERMAN

"Get thee behind me,"
Jesus proclaimed to Peter.
"Stay thine ass there too."

—ERIN JACKSON

There is no god, but
Everybody on the net
Be hashtag blessed yo.

—MARIA BAMFORD

You can always tell
Who went to Catholic school:
They are atheists.

—MIKE BIRBIGLIA

I have learned that, with
Death, it's usually better
To procrastinate.

—JOHN DEBELLIS

Everyone will die.
Not the worst thing. Unless it
Happens all at once.

—LEO ALLEN

What doesn't kill you
Makes you stronger. Unless it's
Mono. Or blood loss.

—JOE ZIMMERMAN

Drunk bike ride at night:

If you romanticize it

It's not dangerous!

—CATHERINE COHEN

Early lasts for hours.

On time lasts a second. Then

You're late. Forever.

—MIKE BIRBIGLIA

The future is now.

No, now. No, wait, now. No now.

Time to reminisce.

—PAUL LANDER

Hindsight is 20

20. But I'll never look

Back on that damn year.

—SASHEER ZAMATA

I've said it before

And I will say it again.

I've said it before.

—ARIEL ELIAS

Asked the universe

To please stop sending me signs.

Has not responded.

—LAURA SILVERMAN

SELF LOVE & LOATHING

Just killed a spider.

Didn't have to, but he saw

Me masturbating.

—RAY ROMANO

I need all of the
Rose quartz and sage you guys have.
My aura is fucked.

—CATHY HUMES

I'm such a Leo

That I don't even believe

In astrology.

—MICHAEL IAN BLACK

People like music
A lot more than comedy.
That makes sense to me.

—KELLY BACHMAN

Saying funny things
Is getting boring for me.
Can I make you cry?

—JEN KIRKMAN

I would kill myself
If I thought it'd make me feel
Better the next day.

—JOHN DEBELLIS

Sometimes I feel like
I'm the only narcissist
In the universe.

—JOSH COMERS

Every person should
Pass a mirror once a day
And say, "damn you cute."

—GIULIA ROZZI

I'm half Taiwanese
Half Japanese. That is why
I look Korean.

—ATSUKO OKATSUKA

How do you know when
You've stopped paying your dues and
Now you're just failing?

—JOSH COMERS

Got so lonely I
Disguised myself and squinted
Into the mirror.

—LEO ALLEN

Historically my

Potential has been untapped

Or not there at all.

—JANEANE GAROFALO

I am thankful for

My superior talent

Which is humbling.

—JOE ZIMMERMAN

Writing haikus can

Make me feel superior.

Prolly cuz I am.

—BETH STELLING

I'm a member of
Eavesdroppers Anonymous.

Not that they know yet.

—MILTON JONES

My therapist thinks

That I'm obsessed with vengeance.

We'll see about that!

—STEWART FRANCIS

My identity

Is not merely in my name.

It is in my bangs.

—ATSUKO OKATSUKA

Started seeing a

Therapist 'cause my parents

Didn't finish me.

—LIZ MIELE

How do you get well

When you are addicted to

Staying on wagons?

—MATTHEW BROUSSARD

The feeling of rage
Is as close as one gets to
Relapsing on coke.

—ROSEBUD BAKER

They tried to make me
Go to rehab and I said
Yeah you're right, good call.

—DAVE HOLMES

All the world's a stage

Except that I have no script

And my lighting sucks.

—COLIN MOCHRIE

Comedy is dumb.

Desperate, insecure people.

I love it so much.

—CHRIS GETHARD

ACKNOWLEDGMENTS

For their personal and professional support, I am eternally grateful to Xenia Mansour, Jeremy Levenbach, Emily Flake, Chris Bannon, Nick Mullendore, Jay Friedenberg, Luke Mansour, Ben Levinsohn, Amy Jacobus, Fred Firestone, Chris Willets, Sam Corbin, Erika Ettin, Ally Spier, Jay Singer, Joanne Sidoti, Son Le, Doug Wihlborg, Carly Miller, Jeffrey Gurian, Beth Lapides, Bruce Smith, Kara Welker, Barry Bookin, George Shapiro, Rory Rosegarten, Steve Gunther, Jodi Lieberman, Amber J. Lawson, and Zoe Friedman, all of whom contributed to this book in ways big and small.

A special note of thanks to Cassidy Graham, my patient and untiring editor, who had a complete vision of this book long before I did; and to Elizabeth Ziman, who knew a good idea when she saw one.

Thanks also to Julie Kim, Scott Koshnoodi, Caitlin Gillette, and the whole Littlefield family for taking an old textile factory and turning it into a place of comedy and community, which fostered this book from conception to completion. (Scott, hope it's not a bust.)

And to Brody, Robin, Mitch, and all others who gave their lives for laughter—thank you.

COMEDY GIVES BACK

All author proceeds from this book will benefit Comedy Gives Back, a nonprofit providing resources for comedians struggling with substance abuse and mental illness, and whose livelihoods have been affected by COVID-19. For information about how to donate, visit comedygivesback .com.

A NOTE FROM THE EDITOR

Any student of poetry will notice a few things wrong with the haikus in this book. Most glaring, perhaps, is the fact that *haiku* is not traditionally pluralized with an *s* (as we've done in the subtitle and in this paragraph). Its plural is simply *haiku*. This was a stylistic choice, and one that many modern haiku poets now favor. Haiku poems also traditionally contain a nature or seasonal word (*kigo*) and a "cutting" word joining two independent thoughts (*kireji*), which most poems in this book do not. Poetic violations such as these are not in ignorance of the haiku rules, but in conscious deviation from them. For these transgressions and others, I must plead artistic liberty.